This *Hurts Me* More Than It Hurts You:

In Words and Pictures

Children Share How Spanking Hurts and What To Do Instead

NADINE A. BLOCK, MEd *with* MADELEINE Y. GOMEZ, PhD

Center for Effective Discipline, 2011

This eye-opening book is written and illustrated by those most affected by spanking—children. Their words and drawings show that spanking doesn't result in the behaviors parents and teachers desire. Instead, it sows seeds of pain, despair, anger, humiliation, confusion, and anger and promotes the continuation of a cycle of violence. The children also share what disciplinary tactics *are* effective. Parents and child-care professionals may be shocked to find that children say reasoned discussions, loss of privileges, time-outs, and the opportunity to atone for misbehaviors work better than spanking.

ABOUT THE EDITORS:

Nadine A. Block, MEd, founded the nonprofit Center for Effective Discipline (CED) in 1987 and served as its executive director until 2010. CED educates the public about physical punishment of children and alternatives; it is also the headquarters of EP-OCH (End Physical Punishment of Children) USA and the NCACPS (National Coalition to Abolish Corporal Punishment in Schools). Block has been a teacher, school psychologist, and consultant to mental-health and child-abuse prevention organizations. In 1998, she initiated SpankOut Day (April 30), which has led to more than twelve thousand parents receiving training in effective, nonviolent alternatives to spanking. A coalition she organized of fifty nonprofit organizations achieved a legislative ban on school corporal punishment in Ohio in 2009. Block is an award-winning, nationally known child advocate. She has been quoted in the *New York Times*, *USA Today*, *Time*, *Family Circle*, *Parenting*, and other periodicals and has appeared on *Larry King Live*, *Good Morning America*, and many other television and radio programs.

Madeleine Y. Gómez, **PhD,** is a licensed clinical psychologist and president of PsycHealth Ltd., a certified minority and women's behavioral health-care organization established in 1989. PsycHealth Ltd. has received URAC Gold and Bronze Awards as well as a Global Communications League of American Communications Professionals Bronze Award. Dr. Gomez is widely respected in her area of specialty—children, families, and abuse. A published researcher, presenter, and assistant professor at Northwestern University, she is also a lifelong human rights advocate. The Southern Poverty Law Center recognized her "outstanding dedication to human rights and equal justice," and the Chicago Board of Education honored her with its Voices of Freedom Award for her work promoting nonviolence and "continuously supporting the self-esteem" of students in Chicago Public Schools. In 2010, Dr. Gomez received the National Psychologist Award from the Dorland Group for her work dedicated to nonviolence, serving the underserved, and promoting quality care.

The editors are parents and grandparents.

CONTENTS

Preface

Part One — Spanking Makes Children Feel…

Chapter 1   Physical Pain… 1
            "I still have marks on my behind."

Chapter 2   Sadness, Depression, Despair… 7
            "Crying and wishing I was never born…"

Chapter 3   Anger and the Cycle of Violence… 13
            "They won't have all that anger stocked up in them."

Chapter 4   Fear, Not Respect… 31
            "Do you really want a child to be so scared?"

Chapter 5   Other feelings… 37
            "I'm concerned about children who are hit by parents
            or teachers."

Part Two — What Children Respond to Instead of Spanking

Chapter 1   What Is Discipline? 45
            "Discipline is about teaching a child right from wrong."

Chapter 2   Taking Away Privileges and Using Time-out… 47
            "Let them think about what they did
            and how they will act better."

Chapter 3   Using Consequences… 51
            "Consequences should be fair."

Chapter 4   Making Amends… 53
            "Community service teaches them to care about others."

Chapter 5   Using Reasoning… 55
            "Talk it over."

Part Three — Resources for Parents and
            Professionals Who Work with Families

Chapter 1   Questions and Answers on Spanking............................61

Chapter 2   Web Sites with Important Information
            about Child Discipline....................................... 65

Chapter 3   Child Discipline Books Worth Reading 67

Chapter 4   Brochures, Handouts, and DVDs on Child Discipline.....71

PREFACE

About 50 percent of U.S. parents report hitting children, whether it is spanking, slapping, whoopin', chastising, whipping, belting, tanning, smacking, paddling, etc. We have so many euphemisms for it that we can barely keep up with them. You can't hit your spouse, your employee, your neighbor, or even your neighbor's dog, but you can still punish your children by hitting them.

The rationale behind hitting children is sometimes based on interpretations of the Bible, claimed to be "discipline," and justified against children, while our laws protect adults. Hitting children has been around for centuries. Hitting slaves and wives used to be legal too, and the Bible was used to support that as well.

A mountain of research from numerous institutions in multiple countries is telling parents to stop hitting children while reporting that it can lead to injury, increased aggression, slower cognitive development, decreased empathy, and mental-health problems. About thirty nations have banned all physical punishment of children in order to reduce child abuse and to give children the right adults have to be protected from physical harm.

Reducing violence against children is the focus of the Center for Effective Discipline, the publisher of this book. Since 1987, the Center's primary goal has been to provide information on the effects of the corporal punishment of children and support positive alternatives in child-rearing. The Center created SpankOut Day April 30, 1998, to bring awareness of this topic to the public.

From this mission, two contests were born. One was an essay contest, and the other was an art contest, both focusing on this issue from the children's point of view. Touching and powerful, the images and words of the children speak for themselves.

Read and learn—Out of the mouths of babes. Look at their courage and honesty in expressing the realities of corporal punishment. May they scatter the seeds of nonviolence wherever they go.

We dedicate this book to the children. We also dedicate this book to you, the reader. In honor of all children, may these words and images of children touch you and support peace and nonviolence in all you do. Truly, the future of our children and our world depends on it.

—Nadine A. Block, MEd, and Madeleine Y. Gómez, PhD

All profits from this book will go to the Center for Effective Discipline to support positive discipline programs for children.

Part 1

Spanking Makes Children Feel...

Drawing by: Girl, Age 10, Kansas

CHAPTER 1

Physical Pain...
"I still have marks on my behind."

Girl, Age 12, Illinois

"I believe spanking is effective because it is painful. Take it from me, I still have marks on my behind...It's not solving the problem because it makes things worse. It makes kids cry. Now, who wants to see their kids cry in pain? Spanking is just wrong! There are other ways to punish your kids. I think parents use this punishment because its quick and easy. Some parents do it for no good reason."

Girl, Age 12, Ohio

"Spanking can hurt children mentally and physically. This causes them to become hurt inside which means they will start abusing others."

Girl, Age 12, Illinois

"When I was a little younger, my mom and dad use to spank me because of bad behavior. I used to be so scared when my parents would spank me. I used to run from spanking and I would be crying. Does it make any sense that I was so scared of a parent that I would choose to run? They always caught me because I was a child and they were quicker than me. I believe that spanking isn't good because kids don't like being hurt...Why, spank your kids if you know how it feels? If you spank kids they might think you hate them or don't love them. They will discipline their children the way they were disciplined. The violence done to kids in the home will never end!"

Drawing by: Girl, Age 9, New York

Girl, Age 14, Philippines

"Every child is unique and special. They have different needs and wants. But they all need love, attention and acceptance of who they are. Children need to be respected, to express their feelings and to be heard. Discipline should not be about punishment. It should be a process of teaching a child right from wrong. Spanking might have a short effect for a child to behave for awhile but through this action parents also teach their children to use violence. And it is not right for any parents or grown-ups to show their love through physical action that could inflict pain."

Boy, Age 12, Illinois

"I believe that spanking isn't good because it teaches children nothing. It doesn't help them, and all it does is hurt them. It is very painful, and might actually make them do more bad things to annoy or disappoint you...Kids are very precious and shouldn't be harmed. No parent would want to be spanked. Why would you want to spank your children?"

Boy, Age 13, Illinois

"Children can get hurt. Parents can hit them too hard and bruise them badly. Then they would be so sore and can't sit down. Then, the child will misbehave in class because of how their parents treat them. The parent will think its ok to hit their kids for no reason. That is a bad influce on their younger siblings and it may cause them to hurt their kids."

Boy, Age 14, Ohio

"Roses are Red. Vilotes are blue. People are abusive don't let it be you. Every night and every day people cry from hands that say—You are bad, You did wrong, and now you pay my way."

Drawing by: Boy, Age 7, South Carolina

Ohio Child (Age Unknown)
BEAT! BEAT! BEAT!

You beat a drum to make music,
You beat eggs to make an omelet
You beat a steak to tenderize it,
You beat clay to mold it,
You let our heart beat to keep you alive,
You beat wisdom into a child's mind through kindness,
But, you don't beat a child to shape or mold.
It doesn't show love.
It doesn't earn respect.
And it doesn't teach.
YOU SHOULD NEVER BEAT A CHILD!!!

Girl, Age 12, Illinois

"...a spanking hurts when your little. When they're older it doesn't hurt as much as it did when they were little. Spankings aren't effective for older children because they sometimes have the courge to talk back to the adult who's giving them a spanking. Talking back to adults is one reason why kids get a spanking...Spanking may be the oldest punishment on earth, but they don't get the job done."

Boy, Age 12, Illinois

"I believe that spankings isn't good for children because it's like a effect that cause a lot of damage to their bottoms, like it turns dark red after a long time you can't sit for a whole hour or so and the belt leaves marks that go right into the skin and has purple where the mark is at."

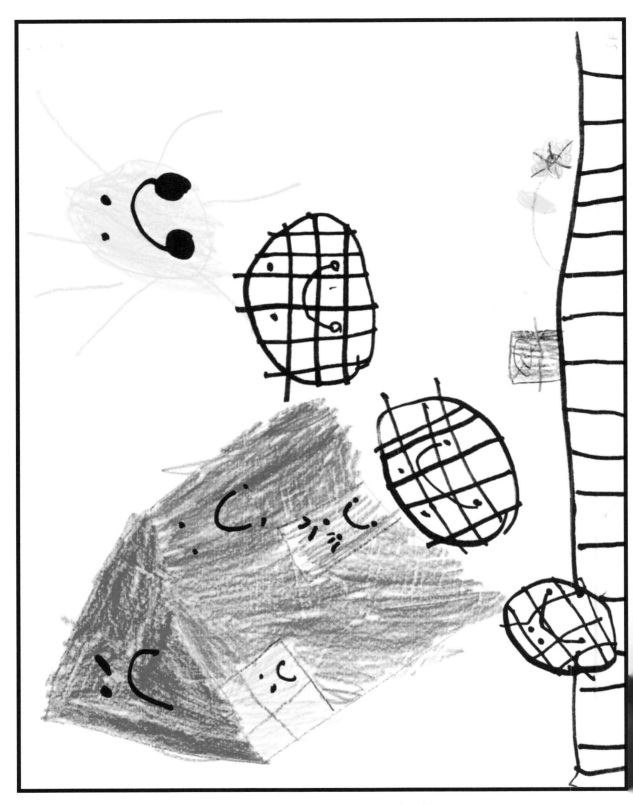

Drawing by: Girl, Age 6, Illinois

CHAPTER 2

Sadness, Depression, Despair...
"Crying and wishing I was never born..."

Drawing by: Girl, Age 7, California

Drawing by: Girl, Age 12, Georgia

Girl, Age 7, Ohio

"Mom yells at me and hits me when she is mad...I wish she would not hit me."

Girl, Age 13, Ohio

"I feel so stupid when I get spanked for things I forget are bad...When my mom hits me, I feel like running away, and I have often planned to run away."

Girl, Age 12, Illinois

"I have seen adults spank their children in public places and other adults just watch. Why wouldn't someone stand up for the child? Would we hit an animal that way in public?"

Girl, Age 13, Illinois

"Say No to Spanking...Parents shouldn't spank their children because it affects your child's feeling. When a child gets a spanking, they only experience the anger their parent has towards them. It makes kids afraid to talk to their parents about their problem because they're afraid of the consequence. Also, spanking can leave marks and bruises on the bodies of innocent children...Spanking is one of the harshest punishments a parent can do to their child. I think parents should think of different ways to deal with family problems other than spanking their kids. Children that are hit will become adults that will hit. We need to try to end this violence so every child can feel safe in his or her home. Let's break the silence!"

Boy, Age 16, Ohio

"Why does he want to hit me? I never do anything bad...I work hard and study and have no friends...I stay out of his way...I feel real bad inside..."

Drawing by: Boy, Age 13, Michigan

Boy, Age 12, Illinois

"Please don't spank me again...it hurts. This is one of the main reasons spankings are bad because anger comes from the person who is spanking you. Sometimes they're angry they might hurt you very seriously. Another thing about spankings is that there comes a time in life when you are to old to get spankings...I've have had many spankings in my life, but I guess my mom finally realized that spanking me would not really solve anything. A spanking is the worst punishment a child can get. My mom hasn't spanked me for a long time. I guess I am more mature then I was when I was younger. Sometimes when I got a spanking, I would still be bad. My mom just stop spanking me, and treats me like an adult. I have a question for all parents. Did you like getting spanked?"

Drawing by: Boy, Age 6, Washington State

CHAPTER 3

Anger and the Cycle of Violence...
"They won't have all that anger stocked up in them."

Boy, Age 14, New Hampshire

"I am 12 years old and I am homeschooled. I am going to tell you a child's perspective of corporal punishment. When I talk about corporal punishment, I'm talking about child abuse because that's exactly what it is. If a husband hits a wife or a wife hits a husband, it's illegal, but if a mother or father hits a child, it's legal. Why is there a difference when two spouses hit each other than when a parent is violent towards a child? What is the difference?

"Some adults like to use the word 'spanking' so the child gets the impression that what the adult is doing is right. But if the adult uses the word 'hit,' the child knows it's wrong. I believe that we need to start calling 'spanking' what it really is: Spanking is HITTING!

"Now I am going to tell you a child's perspective...I was in several foster families. When I was in my biological family I got hit all the time. I also saw my brothers get hit and I hated it. Sometimes at night my stepfather would come in to 'spank' us and we'd all dart under the bed. The only emotion I felt was fear...sheer and utter fear! And sometimes when one of my brothers would do something 'wrong' my birth mother and stepfather would tell me to hit him. I even got hit in one of my foster homes, a place that was supposed to be protecting me from abuse!

"When a child is getting hit, he feels like he is hated and no one loves him. He really feels like no one loves him. Over time, children start putting up bricks around their heart. They start shutting everyone out and they learn to dissociate. When they get older they may become a cold and callous person who can't love. Hitting really does not help their behavior. When people really do tell them wrong from right, they ignore it all. Prisoners may have emotional problems from being hit. Not everyone turns out like that because they may have one person that really loves them.

"When children get hit, the first feeling is fear, 'I'm going to get pain.' It is fear because it means violence. A kid's definition of it is pain. They get that fear that clutches their heart like an iron grip. And that iron grip stays and it hardens over their heart and it just shuts them down. They feel angry, rage. They feel like they just want to get revenge and inflict pain on the one that inflicted pain on them. They feel sadness. The one who gave them the pain is the one who is supposed to protect them from pain. They feel distrust, they can't trust anyone. Their natural feeling when they are with someone who cares is to trust, but when that very person that is supposed to protect them from pain, hurt and sadness hits them, the trust just disappears. They destroy all that trust. Unless someone shows they care who doesn't hurt them, who uses strong but caring words, unless children have that type of person, they are going to stay that way.

"So, if you stop hurting children, then they won't close their heart. They will be more accepting and trusting and they will give that love to another person. They will be more loving so the next generation and then the next and the next will do the same thing. Then there will be peace. If you start with the children a whole chain link starts of love, care, give and take. They won't have all that anger stocked up in them and no one will be angry enough to start wars.

"So you see, to save the world, you need to save the children!"

Drawing by: Boy, Age 12, Connecticut

Drawing by: Girl, Age 11, New Jersey

Girl, Age 13, Illinois

"If you spank kids they might think you hate them or don't love them. They will discipline their children the way they were disciplined. The violence done to kids in the home will never end!"

Drawing by: Girl, Age 10, New Jersey

Girl, Age 11, North Carolina

Spark

It started as just a spark.
Just a simple "Go to your room!"
If only they had went.
But they chose to play with first.
Wood first.
A "no" would have to do.
A stronger voice...
Then came the gasoline.
A spark that fueled a war
A hit that blew a scream
A pound that burned the comfort
And only one could wish to restore
A log cabin
Burned
With just one spark.
So here I lay,
Only saying the dearest words
That would rip me apart
Ones that would scream
For me to mend them.
But I couldn't.
I just couldn't move.
I ran from you
Ran from reality
You didn't have to burn me down
For me to just apologize

You didn't have to tell me to "shut up!"
For me to just say that I was sorry.
But you did need to hurt me
To send me off crying and wishing
I was never born.
And so this spark
Grew into something much more
A wildfire

This spark
It burned down
Hopes and dreams
And a gentle feeling
The most important one.
This spark.

Boy, Age Unknown, Ohio

"Little kids they do not know right from wrong. I no you have to discipline kids but people get to carried away. Why do people have to beat their kids with their bare hand. To mom's and dad's that whip their kids. You know you can break a babys bones or kill them from beating them. So why do you do it...that's the question. Just look in to their eye's before you raise your hand. That 'sad puppy dog' look can make me cry. So how can you use your fist, or a switch to hit a kid...please! stop child abuse because if you abuse your kids, their going to abuse kids. But if you stop the abuse now and find a new way to discipline child the cycle of abuse will stop."

Drawing by: Girl, Age 12, Virginia

Drawing by: Girl, Age 9, Arizona

Girl, Age 14, Illinois

"Parents know kids don't like getting spanked, and it seems like they don't care...Adults can teach children without spanking. It's easy. Just talk to them and find another consequence for the mistake they made. Every child needs to feel safe in their homes and know they won't be hurt physically. The message needs to get out in every neighborhood of this great country. Let's get this done together."

Girl, Age 15, Ohio

I had a little sister
I was so happy then
I had a little sister
She had a pretty grin
I had a little sister
I was so happy then
Oh how we laughed and played
Her eyes twinkled when she would see me
I had a little sister
I was so happy then
Until my mommy shook her
Now the happiness is gone
I have no little sister
She has a face of stone
I had a little sister
I was so happy then
Her eyes no longer twinkle
She will never see me again
I have no little sister
The happiness is gone

She will never laugh
I will always cry with every thought of her
Did you know I had a little sister?
Until my mommy shook her!!!

Drawing by: Girl, Age 10, Washington State

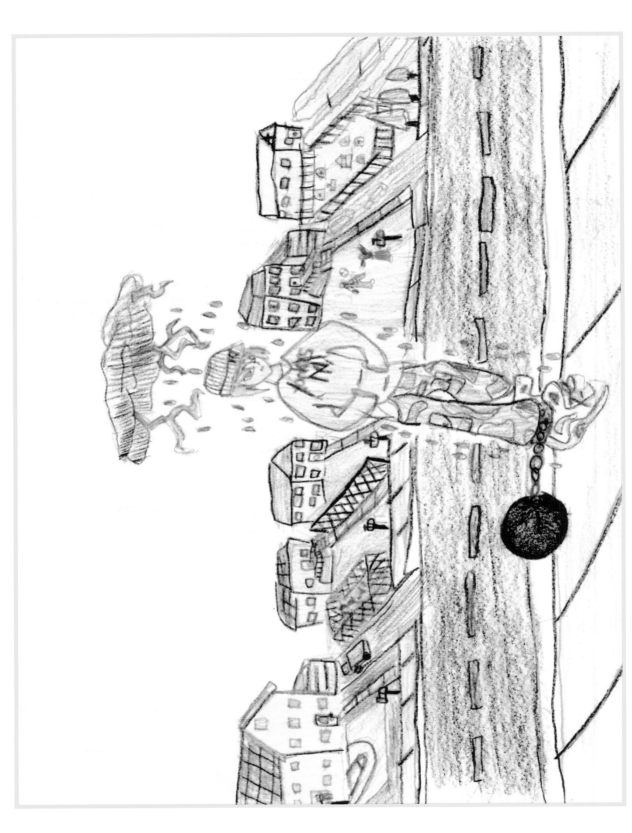

Drawing by: Boy, Age 12, New Jersey

Girl, Age 13, Ohio

"Spanking is harmful and emotional for you and your child. When spanking a child, it makes them feel like they are powerless. Spanking makes a child feel like something is wrong with them, instead of their behavior. It can be emotional for parents also. After spanking a child it could lead to remorse and guilt...Spanking is a very bad thing."

Boy, Age 13, Illinois

"Many adults spank their children. Sometimes they think it is the best way to punish a child. I believe spanking isn't effective because all you're doing is hitting a child. When I get a spanking (mainly from my mom) it dosen't hurt...it just makes me very mad...It can give a kid violent thoughts...Everyone should stop harsh spankings on kids."

Girl, Age 13, Illinois

"Some people say that spanking is a form of discipline and a training of respect...Spanking should be the last resort. Spanking affects different people different ways. Spanking makes some kids angry and that makes kids do the opposite of what you tell them to do. Other children get depressed and become quiet. The last expression I know that a child gets after a spanking is annoyance. Annoyance means that they are short-tempered and the smallest things get them angry. I know all these things because I get like that after I'm spanked. I don't think that I will spank my kids when I grow up, but I won't let them get away with certain things. Spanking is a bad thing because it affects everyone."

Girl, Age 14, Philippines

"When a child commits a mistake or misbehave, I firmly believe spanking is not the solution. It will only make a child more aggressive and angry. I believe communication plays an important role in order to discipline a child. It is important for parents and grownups to encourage a child to talk, to open up to them to understand and handle the situation properly."

Drawing by: Girl, Age 10, Florida

26

Boy, Age Unknown, Ohio

Children Make Mistakes

Don't hit your children
Because if you do they
Will hit on their children.
Why do you have to beat your children?
Were they bad?
Does anyone deserve to be beaten?
If you treat your children with respect,
They will learn to respect you and others.
All children make mistakes
They don't need a beating.
They need a consequence for misbehavior.
No one deserves to be beaten.
If they are beaten,
They become mean and angry at the world.

Boy, Age 13, Illinois

"Spanking as I see it is a way parents release their anger they have on their child. It sometimes seems like they're enjoying it because of their facial expressions and the way they sound. That's just how they are at times. Also spanking shouldn't be used on kids at any age. When you spank your children they learn violence is needed to solve a problem. Parents should be teaching their children how to solve problems without violence."

Drawing by: Girl, Age 8, New York

28

Girl, Age 14, Illinois

"Too many parents think that spanking is a good way for parents to teach children a lesson or teach manners. When some children get in trouble, they see a belt or a hand coming their way. I used to get whooping all the time when I was young, but now I don't. I remember the pain that a spanking caused and the anger I felt after the punishment... If parents want their children to grow up to be peacemakers, then they need to see their parents fix a negative situation. Showing the violence will only make the situation worse."

Boy, Age 12, Illinois

"The bad part about spanking is that your parents do it to you thinking that you will obay them for now on, and a lot of kid's seem like they become more angry and bader after a spanking. Another thing about it is bad because some parent's want there child to be perfact, so for an example some kid's bring home one a, on a test but a c- on another and there parent spank's them because they have a c- ."

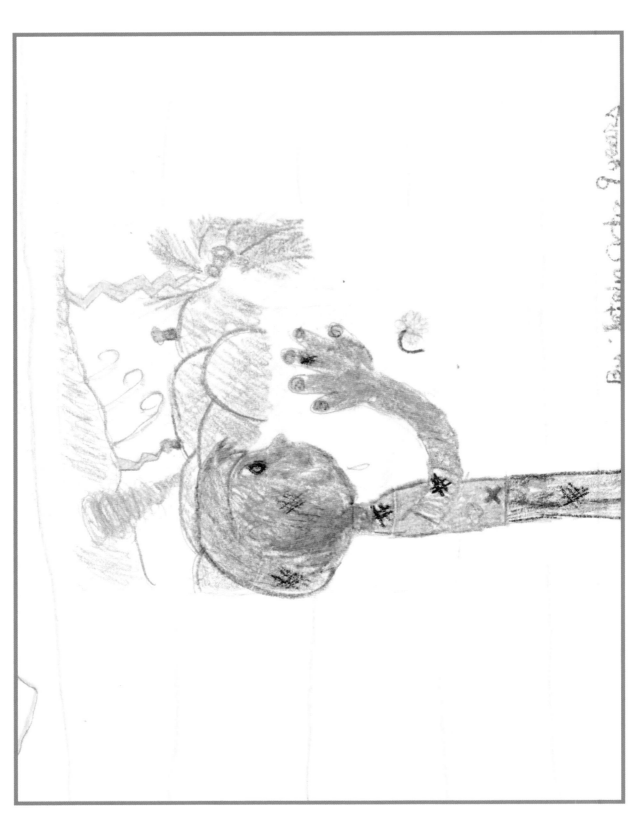

Drawing by: Girl, Age 9, Puerto Rico

CHAPTER 4

Fear, Not Respect...
"Do you really want a child to be so scared?"

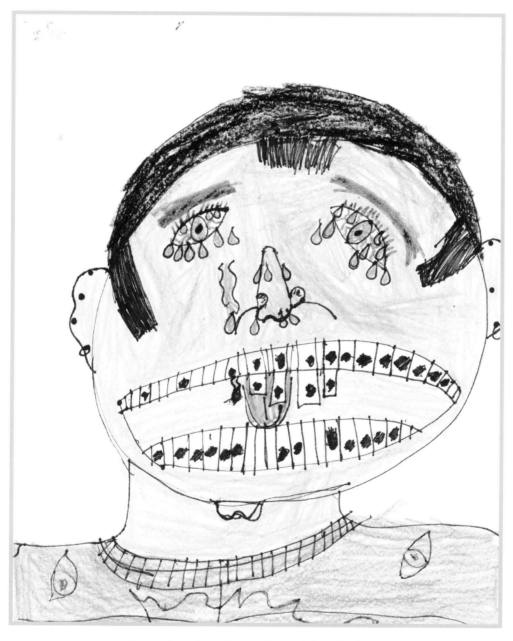

Drawing by: Boy, Age 10, Virginia

Boy, Age 14, Ohio

"Kids in the United states today are afraid of being spanked. This causes these kids to be afraid of their own parents...The children who are being spanked may think they are being beaten. This causes these kids to think their whole life that they grew up being beaten by their parents...Many kids are afraid to do anything around their parents without the fear of being spanked...They start to believe their parents don't love them or like them anymore."

Girl, Age 13, Ohio

"Do you really want a child to be scared when they make a mistake or would you rather have them learn something from it. Once the spanking is over it's easy to forget what they even got in trouble for. The punishment is just too quick. The child doesn't even have time to think about the mistake they made...Would you like to be spanked? No, of course not."

Girl, Age 12, Illinois

"Spanking isn't effective because it creates fear rather than punishment. When parents spank children, they try to teach obedience, but not to make them understand what they did was wrong. Spankings are really used to harm the children instead of correcting the behavior. Parents also shouldn't do it because it makes children think that parents want to hurt them...When a child is spanked, they feel pain for a while but they still don't correct the problem."

Boy, Age 13, Illinois

"I believe spanking isn't effective because when children grow up, they would remember how horrible they would get a whooping. A lot of parents beat on their children for no apparent reason. They feel it is a quick way to solve problems. I don't believe that any problems can be solved with violence...If parents want their children to grow up to be peacemakers, then they need to set examples for their kids. Their kids need to see their parents problem solve to fix a negative situation. Showing the violence will only make a situation worse."

Drawing by: Girl, Age 9, Arizona

Drawing by: Boy, Age 7, South Carolina

Girl, Age 12, Ohio

"...spanking can drive your kids away from you. This can happen if you spank your child for any reason at all. It only takes one time for things to get out of control, and you can make it so your kids won't want anything to do with you."

Boy, Age 12, Illinois

"I believe spanking isn't good because it can bruse children inside and out and, make them angry. Its also very painful and makes them afraid. I believe that if children are afraid of adults they won't have open discusion with the parent."

Spankings HURT!!

I think spankings are embarrassing because you get laughed at if you're spanked in public.

Drawing by: Boy, Age 7, South Carolina

CHAPTER 5

Other Feelings
"I'm concerned about children
who are hit by parents or teachers."

Boy, Age 9, California

"I am 9 years old...I am worried that children may still be paddled in schools in many parts of the United States. I know spanking is painful and humiliating. No child deserves to be paddled. I am fortunate that my parents have never spanked me or my brother. However, other children do live in families that spank, and attend schools where paddling is common. My parents have asked me to donate to a small number of deserving charities. Each year, I select a few that I believe are particularly worthy. I have chosen to continue to support your organization because of the fine work that you do for children. I would like my donation to support your organization's mission."

"Sometimes talking doesn't work."

Boy, Age 13, Illinois

"Here are reasons why spanking is good, one if you spank your kids that can mean you can have control over them if they don't listen to you. Or if you always talk to them when they did wrong and that didn't work, then to me it will be ok to spank your child. Sometimes talking to them isn't always going to work because they will keep doing the same thing over and over again. My mom used to always spank if I will do wrong.

She would try talking to me and if that didn't get through my mind she would pull out the belt."

"Spanking and whooping are different."

Girl, Age 13, Illinois

"...do you think spanking is a good way to disaplend your child, or any child? Well, if you don't, I do. Spanking to me should be used for kids of the ages 4–7. I say this because, when you are still young, you really don't be as aware to your actions as when you get older. You should only give a child a spanking at this age to let them relize that what they did was wrong. At the ages 8–17, or at least when you are still under your parents roof you should get a wooping. A wooping is when your parent gets a belt and you lay on your stomach and they hit your behind with a belt. Now this is when it gets a little more serious. I say this because when you are at least 8 or 9 years of age, you show know whats right and whats wrong. A spanking is just a little tap to me, but a wooping is a different story. If you give a teenager or a preteen a spanking, they would just take advantage of it. If you woop them and show them that you mean what you say, then I guanarntee that whatever they did they will not do it again. Whatever punishment the parents give to their child is a punishment of their choice. Just don't forget that spanking and wooping are two different things, and it really depends on the age of the child. Disaplend is never a bad thing for a child."

Embarrassment: Public Spankings Are Embarrassing

Boy, Age Unknown, Ohio

"I think that the pro of spanking is that you can teach your child a lesson...I don't feel like you should beat your child, but I feel like you should tap them on their hands or on their behind as the last resource.

Hard enough to enable your purpose and not hurt them. If you start young, they will learn I think that the cons of spanking your child is that you might be out in public and your child does something out of place and you spank them. Somebody might see you and call children services on you. Or your child might grow up thinking that you don't love them. That's why you should tell them the reason why they are getting a spanking. Another thing is that if your child bruise easy and you leave marks that could also be a problem."

Boy, Age 14, Illinois

"I was watching a show called *The Supernanny* and the parents would spank the child every time they did something wrong. The children didn't respond to the spanking as the parents thought they would. I mean that the spanking did no good. They did the same thing over again."

Girl, Age 13, Illinois

"A spanking is striking a child with your hand or an object. This term sounds like something that should be done to an untamed animal, not a child. So why do some parents use this ineffective form of discipline? Parents may say it's useful, but I strongly disagree with them. Discipline means to punish in order to correct or train. The last time I checked parents don't train children, except to go to the washroom as babies."

"Sad and Angry at the Same Time"
Drawing by: Girl, Age 10, Ohio

Drawing by: Girl, Age 9, Alabama

Part 2

What Children Respond to
Instead of Spanking

"Discipline means to teach."
Drawing by: Girl, Age 12, North Carolina

CHAPTER 1

What Is Discipline?
"Discipline is about teaching a child right from wrong."

Girl, Age 14, Philippines

"Each child is unique and special...Children need to be respected, to express their feelings and to be heard. Discipline should not be about punishment. It should be a process of teaching a child right from wrong. Spanking might have a short effect for the child to behave for a while but through this action parents also teach their children to use violence. And it is not right for any parents or grown-ups to show their love through physical action that could inflict pain...Positive discipline works for me. Like if I want something, I have to earn it. I have to keep my grades high, keep my room clean, and be responsible in everything I do. Every Sunday, my mom makes it a point that it is a family day. My parents listen to what we have to say and give us advised. They will constantly remind us that we have a choice between what is good and what is bad. And if we did something wrong, we have to have the courage to admit it and promise ourselves not to commit the same mistake. They are not happy if we misbehave but constantly remind us that they love us. My mom is always calm and patient and very specific with the house rule. My parents make us feel secured and loved."

Girl, Age 14, Ohio

"Discipline is a very good way of resolving problems. Spanking a child does not build them up, but tears them down. The word discipline comes

45

from the Greek word, disciple, which means to teach something of value. Good discipline should strengthen the child parent relationship and be able to encourage the child to learn skills and also build a strong bond with their mom and dad. An alternative to violence would be to allow the child to make mistakes and then help them in finding solutions to their different problems.

"When I make mistakes my parents will say, 'Well what are you going to do about it?' Sometimes they will force me to think for myself. That tells me they think I can do it. Whenever I think my parents think so highly of me, it makes me feel real good!"

Boy, Age 12, Illinois

"To show your child love, treat them with respect. Spanking only causes pain. It doesn't show love."

CHAPTER 2

Taking Away Privileges and Using Time-out…
"Let them think about what they did and
how they will act better."

Girl, Age 12, Illinois

"Adults can teach children without spanking by putting them in timeout or taking away their toys or privileges. Anything but spanking is fine with me. Adults need to calm their angry by doing some deep breathing. Instead of taking it out on there kids. Can we get a break? All I'm trying to say is don't hit your children. Do a little tap on their hand every once in a while. Just don't get the big belt and hit your kids. It doesn't solve any problems."

Girl, Age 13, Ohio

"Spanking can hurt children mentally and physically. This causes them to become hurt inside which means they will start abusing others. I am going to talk about a couple ways that you can discipline your child without hurting them. One way is to send them to their room. This will give them time to relax and think about what they have done wrong. Then call them down and tell them some reasons why by taking away privileges. This could help by letting them know that if you make a bad choice, things could be eliminated in your life. These are some good reasons why spanking is not a good thing to make your child go through. If you follow what's right, spanking will be eliminated in your life."

Drawing by: Girl, Age 6, Illinois

Boy, Age 13, Illinois

"Adults can teach children without spanking by using punishments or just talking to them. The way my parents punish me is by taking my video games and my cell phone to. Now, that's a punishment because I love my phone. Right now I don't have my phone because of a punishment."

Girl, Age 14, Illinois

"For as long as I can remember, I have been raised like a young lady. I never have gotten a spanking. I always get punishments because the Bible says 'train up a child in the way they should go.' There's no reason to spank your child, even if he or she has done wrong. Parents should find something that the child values most, and take it away from him. You can also try and discuss the situation with their child. They should try and get in your childs mind and see what's going on in their life. That's why I believe that a child getting a spanking is not a good thing."

Girl, Age 12, Illinois

"Adults can teach children without spanking by taking privileges away from them. They can talk to them about what is right and wrong. These talks will help children when they are involved in a situation that could involve them making a bad decision. You want your kids to be prepared to make good choices so that they don't need punishments. I pray that spanking isn't allowed in the future."

Girl, Age 13, Illinois

"Adults can teach children without spanking. It's easy. Just talk to them and find another consequence for the mistake they made. If a parent takes away a toy or privilege, the same message that the spanking would give could be done without harsh punishment. If parent are having a hard time disciplining their child, they could bring in other family members. These family members could assist the family in an action plan to help improve behavior. Remember: It takes a village to raise a child."

Drawing by: Girl, 13, India

CHAPTER 3

Using Consequences...
"Consequences should be fair."

Boy, Age 12, Ohio

"There are many different ways to discipline your children. Some parents ground their kids. When you ground your kids most parents put their child into their rooms and take away privileges like games, TV, and using the phone. When you do this, it is supposed to let your kids sit in their rooms and think about what they did and how they will act better. Another way to discipline your children is to make them write lines. Some parents make their kids sit down and write about what they did and how they will act better the next time something like this happens. This is supposed to make your kids not want to write and make them think before they do it again. These are both good ways of disciplining your children. It gets the same idea across and it does not hurt your children. So the next time you think about spanking your kids remember the other ways to discipline your kids and <u>do not spank them</u>."

Boy, Age 12, Illinois

"People need to show their child consequences when they don't follow the rules. These consequences need to be fair and not involve hitting. Families need to work together not to spank their children and find alternate consequences. So, if you are ever in a situation of spanking, just talk it out and you all both get an understanding. This is the best way not to cause conflict...I know that when I am adult, I will never use spanking as a form of discipline."

Boy, Age 14, Illinois

"I think instead of spanking, another consequence the parents should give the kids is take away all of their privileges, such as, their TV, their games, their phone, going outside and playing with friends. They should stay in their room (locked) grounded for a couple of months until they get tired of looking at the paint on their wall."

Girl, Age 13, Illinois

"Sometimes kids have to learn on our own by doing mistakes and not always have parents up on our backs, blinded by whippings. In some situations instead of spanking you could always communicate so that way you can get your point across, but at the same time grow your relationship."

CHAPTER 4

Making Amends...
"Community service teaches them to care about others."

Drawing by: Boy, Age 12, Pennsylvania

Girl, Age 12, Ohio

"Community service benefits the town and gives the child time to think of what they did wrong. It also teaches them to care about others. Some service they could perform would be helping out at a nursing home, food pantry or thrift store. A punishment like this that takes them away from there usual activities, might make them think twice about misbehaving at school. In conclusion, I believe spanking is unhelpful in preventing bad behavior. Let's turn a negative into a positive. No more spanking."

CHAPTER 5

Using Reasoning…
"Talk it over."

Drawing by: Girl, Age 8, Illinois

Girl, Age Unknown, Ohio

"In today's society many adults use physical discipline as a tool to teach children what is right vs. what is wrong. Yet, I as a teenager believe there is a better way to teach children right or wrong without using physical contact. A better way to teach a child would be to talk to him or her. Find out what their true feelings are and why they do the things they do. For example, a ten-year old girl or boy sneaks into his or her mothers purse. He or she then takes ten dollars out of the wallet that was in the purse. The mother finds out. She spanks the child. Next the mom explans to the child why he or she was spanked. This is a negative in my eyes because physical contact such as spanking could lead to violence. Also, the same point could have been made with out spanking or touching the child."

Boy, Age 12, Illinois

"Adults can teach their children without spanking by giving them a set of rules to follow and then know what will happen if they don't follow the rules. Parents should also set good examples for their children by always telling them the truth and trying to give them rewards when they stay on task."

Boy, Age 11, Illinois

"There are other ways of teaching your child to behave. You can talk to them in private. If they aren't doing well in school make them stay...so they can get help. If needed sign them up for tutoring after school. You can stop them from watching tv for a month. You can take games for a month. You can make him not have company or sleepovers...You will think about how you will talk to him. You will be calm while talking to him. You will listen to what they have to say."

Boy, Age 12, Illinois

"Adults can teach children without spanking them by helping them. They can also talk to them somewhere quiet. They can also tell them to try hard or better next time. Adults can also tell them stuff they shouldn't do. Parents need to be involved in there child's life and then there won't be need for spankings...I pray they talk to their children. I think adults will be made if they got a spanking, so why should they do it to us?"

Girl, Age 12, Illinois

"Adults can teach children without spankings by not getting mad at them like if they have a upcoming test on spelling or a vocabulary. They should help them study so they can get a really impressive grade on it to avoid the spankings. Everything doesn't have to be solved with a spanking just help them study and don't get too mad at them and give them harsh punishment. I mean like how come we can't get a break from spankings?"

Girl, Age 13, Illinois

"I have a question for all the parents. Did you like getting spanked? Well I would hope not but your children don't like get spanked just like when you were little. So just try my advice and you and your child will have a better life."

Drawing by: Girl, Age 12, South Carolina

Part 3

Resources for Parents and Professionals Who Work with Families

CHAPTER 1

Questions and Answers on Spanking

(Q) What is spanking?
Spanking means to hit a child on the buttocks with the flat of the hand or an instrument to stop or prevent misbehavior. *Spanking* is a form of corporal punishment.

(Q) What is corporal punishment?
Corporal punishment is the intentional infliction of physical pain to stop or prevent misbehavior. It includes spanking; hitting children with instruments, such as belts or whips; twisting or pulling arms or ears; and forcing them to stand or kneel in uncomfortable positions for a long time. *Physical punishment* is a synonym for corporal punishment.

(Q) Is spanking legal?
All states have statutes or court decisions that permit parents to use physical punishment as long as it is reasonable force that is reasonably necessary to maintain discipline or promote the child's welfare. A parent is likely to be investigated by police or child protection authorities if physical injury is evident. Judges and juries determine whether children have been physically abused according to their interpretation of state laws.

Nineteen states permit corporal punishment in schools. Corporal punishment in schools generally means "paddling," which involves an educator hitting a child on the buttocks with a board usually eighteen to twenty-four inches long, an inch thick, and three to four inches wide, for breaking school rules. Within the nineteen states that allow school corporal punishment, local school districts are permitted to ban it and, in most cases, regulate how it is used. States where corporal punishment is *not* permitted are: Alaska, California, Connecticut, Delaware, District of Columbia, Hawaii, Illinois, Iowa, Maine, Maryland, Massachusetts, Michigan, Minnesota, Montana, Nebraska, New Mexico, Nevada, New Hampshire, New Jersey, New York, North Dakota, Ohio, Oregon, Pennsylvania, Rhode Island, South Dakota, Utah, Vermont, Virginia, Washington, West Virginia, and Wisconsin.

See state laws on: "Differentiating Child Abuse from Parental Corporal Punishment and Reasonable Parental Discipline," American Bar Association Center for Children and the Law Center for Effective Discipline, **http://www.stophitting.com/index.php?page=punishvsabuse** (accessed February 2011).

For current state laws on school corporal punishment see: "Discipline and the Law," Center for Effective Discipline, **http://www.stophitting. com/index.php?page=legalinformation** (accessed March 2011).

A majority of states ban corporal punishment in state-regulated day care, child-care centers, foster homes, and institutions. Center for Effective Discipline, 2008, **http://www.stophitting.com/index. php?page=statelegislation** (accessed March 2011).

(Q) What is discipline?

1. Discipline is helping a child develop self-control by teaching, guiding, and explaining about what was wrong with the child's behavior and what to do instead.

2. It involves setting limits and correcting misbehavior quickly and in respectful ways, like using verbal redirection or even a raised eyebrow.

3. It means being consistent and firm but also kind and fair.

4. It is about providing a trusting and loving atmosphere, teaching children to make good choices, and being a good model for them.

5. For infants and toddlers, it means supervision and being alert to early signs of trouble, distracting them or removing them from situations, redirecting their behavior, and safety-proofing their environment.

6. Discipline can also involve "restitution." For example, if a child does something that violates the rights of a sibling, he or she should be told, "Since you purposely did xxx to your sister, you need to apologize and do something nice for her to make up for what you did. Tonight, you should do her household chore in addition to your own."

7. Rewards work better than punishments in changing behaviors.

From: Center for Effective Discipline Parent Resources, **http://www. stophitting.com** (accessed February, 2011).

(Q) Is spanking harmful?

Almost all research shows that spanking is harmful and ineffective in the long term in changing behavior. Parents often think corporal punishment "works" because it stops misbehavior momentarily.

The Report on Physical Punishment in the United States: What Research Tells Us about Its Effects on Children, authored by Elizabeth T. Gershoff, PhD, brings together over one hundred years of social science research and dozens of published studies on physical punishment conducted by professionals in the fields of education, psychology, medicine, sociology, and child development. The report is endorsed by major organizations, such as the American Medical Association, the American Academy of Pediatrics, and the National PTA.

Among findings on effects of corporal punishment from this report:

- Physical punishment, when administered regularly, increases antisocial behavior, such as lying, stealing, cheating, bullying, assaulting a sibling or peers, and lack of remorse for wrongdoing.

- Physical punishment increases the risk of child abuse.

- Physical punishment serves as a model for aggressive behavior and for inappropriate ways of dealing with conflict.

- Physical punishment erodes trust between a parent and child.

- Physical punishment adversely affects cognitive development.

- Adults who were hit frequently as children are likely to suffer from depression and other negative social and mental health outcomes.

Contact the Center for Effective Discipline for information about copies of this report at **Info@stophitting.org**.

CHAPTER 2

Web Sites with Important Information about Child Discipline

American Academy of Pediatrics

"Healthy Children Communication and Discipline."
http://www.healthychildren.org/English/family-life/family-dynamics/ communication-discipline/Pages/default.aspx (accessed July 2011).

American Humane Association

"Child Discipline."
http://www.americanhumane.org/about-us/newsroom/fact-sheets/ child-discipline.html (accessed July 2011).

American Psychological Association

"Violence Prevention for Families of Young Children and Understanding Child Development as a Violence Prevention Tool."
http://www.ACTAgainstViolence.org (accessed July 2011).

Ask Dr. Sears.com

Parent questions and answers on parenting issues including discipline, **http://www.askdrsears.com/** (accessed July 2011).

Attachment Parenting International

Many printouts on discipline of children of all ages, **http://www.attachmentparenting.org/** (accessed July 2011).

Center for Effective Discipline

Information on the effects of physical punishment and state-by-state laws on school corporal punishment and differentiating child abuse from reasonable corporal punishment. The site also has available parent resource and training materials on discipline, **http://www.stophitting.org** (accessed July 2011).

"Religion and Spanking."
http://www.stophitting.com/index.php?page=religion-main (accessed July 2011).

Global Initiative to End All Corporal Punishment of Children

Information about international laws and progress in ending all corporal punishment of children,
http://www.endcorporalpunishment.org/ (accessed July 2011).

Nemours Children's Hospital

Kids Health from Nemours: "Disciplining Your Child."
http://kidshealth.org/parent/positive/talk/discipline.html (accessed July 2011).

Parents and Teachers against Violence in Education (PTAVE)

Campaigns against corporal punishment of children in all settings,
http://www.nospank.net/ (accessed July 2011).

Parents Anonymous

The oldest child abuse prevention organization in the U.S. Materials for parents and parent training opportunities,
http://www.parentsanonymous.org/ (accessed July 2011).

Religious Tolerance

"Religion and Spanking."
http://www.religioustolerance.org/spankin10.htm (accessed July 2011).

The Natural Child Project

The Natural Child Project: Articles on gentle guidance.
http://www.naturalchild.org (accessed July 2011).

CHAPTER 3

Child Discipline Books Worth Reading

Agassi, Martine, and Marieka Heinlen. 2006. *Hands Are Not for Hitting*. Minneapolis, MN: Free Spirit Publishing Inc. [Note: a book for children or parents to read to children.]

Bailey, Becky. 2002. *Easy to Love, Difficult to Discipline: The Seven Basic Skills for Turning Conflict into Cooperation*. New York: HarperCollins Publishers Inc.

Faber, Adele, and Elaine Mazlish. 1980. *How to Talk So Kids Will Listen, and Listen So Kids Will Talk*. New York: Avon Books, **http://www.fabermazlish.com/Books.htm** (accessed July 2011).

———. 2005. *How to Talk So Teens Will Listen and Listen So Teens Will Talk*. New York: HarperCollins Publishers Inc., **http://www.fabermazlish.com/Books.htm** (accessed July 2011).

Gordon, Thomas, PhD. 2000. *Parent Effectiveness Training, P.E.T. Book*. Book, DVDs, workshop information, **http://dev.gordontraining.com/parent-programs/parent-effectiveness-training-p-e-t/** (accessed July 2011).

Greene, Ross. 2005. *The Explosive Child: A New Approach for Understanding and Parenting Easily Frustrated, Chronically Inflexible Children*. New York: HarperCollins Publishers Inc.

Karp, Harvey. 2004. *The Happiest Toddler on the Block: How to Eliminate Tantrums and Raise a Patient, Respectful, and Cooperative One- to Four-Year-Old*. Revised Ed. New York: Bantam Dell.

Kirkland, Asadah. 2009. *Beating Black Kids*. New York: Asadah Sense Consulting Publisher, **http:www.beatingblackkids.com** (accessed July 2011)

Kvols, Kathryn. 1997. *Redirecting Children's Behavior*. Seattle: Parenting Press. Courses are available and instructors are certified by the International Network for Children and Families. Videotapes and online courses are available at: **http://www.incaf.com/coursesforparents.html** (accessed July 2011).

Nelsen, Jane, EdD, Cheryl Erwin, MA, and Roslyn Ann Duffy. 2007. *Positive Discipline for Preschoolers: For Their Early Years—Raising Children who Are Responsible, Respectful, and Resourceful*. New York: Three Rivers Press.

———. 1998. *Positive Discipline: The First Three Years: From Infant to Toddler—Laying the Foundation for Raising a Capable, Confident Child*. Roseville, CA: Prima Publishing.

Nelsen, Jane, EdD, Lynn Lott, and H. Stephen Glenn. 2007. *Positive Discipline A–Z: 1001 Solutions to Everyday Parenting Problems*. New York: Three Rivers Press.

Samalin, Nancy, and Catherine Whitney. 2003. *Loving without Spoiling and 100 Other Timeless Tips for Raising Terrific Kids*. New York: McGraw-Hill Companies.

Shure, Myrna B. 2005. *Thinking Parent, Thinking Child: How to Turn Your Most Challenging Everyday Problems into Solutions*. New York: McGraw-Hill.

Books, Studies, and Reports about the Effects of Physical Punishment of Children

Durrant, Joan, PhD, and Anne B. Smith, PhD. 2010. *Global Pathways to Abolishing Physical Punishment: Realizing Children's Rights*. New York: Routledge. (A book about the progress being made worldwide in recognizing children's rights and ending the physical punishment of children.)

Farmer, Alice. 2009. *A Violent Education: Corporal Punishment of Children in U.S. Public Schools*. Human Rights Watch and American Civil Liberties Union (report), **http://www.aclu.org/human-rights-racial-justice/violent-education-corporal-punishment-children-us-public-schools** (accessed July 2011).

Gershoff, Elizabeth. T. 2008. *The Report on Physical Punishment in the United States: What Research Tells Us about Its Effects on Children*. Columbus, OH: Center for Effective Discipline. The report is endorsed by major organizations, such as the American Medical Association, the American Academy of Pediatrics, and the National PTA., **http://www.phoenixchildrens.com/community/injury-prevention-center/effective-discipline.html** (accessed July 2011).

———. 2002. "Parental Corporal Punishment and Associated Child Behaviors and Experiences: A Meta-analytic and Theoretical Review." *Psychological Bulletin* 128, 539–579. (study.)

Greven, Philip. 1991. *Spare the Child: The Religious Roots of Punishment and the Psychological Impact of Physical Abuse*. New York: Random House. (book.)

Greydanus, Donald. E., et. al. 2003. Corporal Punishment in Schools: Position Paper of the Society for Adolescent Medicine. *Journal of Adolescent Health* 32, no. 5, 385–393. (study.)

Straus, Murray A. 2001. *Beating the Devil out of Them: Corporal Punishment in American Families*. 2nd ed. Piscataway, NJ: Transaction Publishers. (book.)

CHAPTER 4

Brochures, Handouts, and DVDs on Child Discipline

Active Parenting USA
Books, videos, CDs, parenting workshops, and leader training are available from the Active Parenting USA Headquarters, Kennesaw, Georgia. Spanish materials are also available,
http://www.activeparenting.com/ (accessed July 2011).

Attachment Parenting International
Effective Discipline: Positive Discipline, Discipline through Play, and More
A brochure from Attachment Parenting International,
http://www.attachmentparenting.org/parentingtopics/ effectivediscipline.php (accessed July 2011).

Center for Effective Discipline
Are Discipline and Spanking the Same Thing? Printout with self-test from the Center for Effective Discipline,
http://www.stophitting.com/index.php?page=thesame (accessed July 2011).

Ten Reasons for Not Hitting Children
A handout from the Center for Effective Discipline,
http://www.stophitting.com/index.php?page=10reasons2 (accessed July 2011).

Children's Hospitals and Clinics of Minneapolis/St Paul
Positive Discipline: A Guide for Parents
Children's Hospitals and Clinics of Minneapolis/St. Paul (2009). Download available at:
http://www.childrensmn.org/web/healthprof/027121.pdf (accessed July 2011).

Children's Hospital of Philadelphia
General Principles of Discipline
Children's Hospital of Philadelphia (CHOP) Download available at:
http://www.chop.edu/healthinfo/general-principles-of-discipline.html
(accessed July 2011).

Family Development Resources
The Power of Positive Parenting—I'm Only Doing This for Your Own Good
A DVD from the series on alternatives to spanking, which is available
through Family Development Resources. Other materials are available
on the Web site:
http://www.nurturingparenting.com/npp/pdfs/catalog_all_programs. pdf (accessed July 2011).

Jane Bluestein PhD Instructional Support Services, Inc.
Simple and Practical Steps to Using Positive Discipline with Young Children
A brochure from Jane Bluestein,
http://www.safechildnc.org/media/pdf/parenting_resources/ discipline_brochure.pdf (accessed July 2011).

Katherine Kersey EdD
101 Positive Principles of Discipline
Katharine Kersey, Professor of Early Childhood Education at Old
Dominion University, Richmond, Virginia,
http://www.odu.edu/~kkersey/101s/101principles.shtml (accessed July
2011). Other materials are available on the Web site.

Kids Are Worth It!
Free handouts from Barbara Coloroso on the discipline of children,
such as "Parenting and Teaching with Wit and Wisdom." Other
materials are available on the Web site:
http://www.kidsareworthit.com/Handouts.html (accessed July 2011).

Parents and Teachers Against Violence in Education (PTAVE)
Plain Talk about Spanking
A brochure by Jordan Riak,
http://nospank.net/pt2009.htm (accessed July 2011).

The Power of Peace
A brochure by Mitch Hall and Madeleine Y. Gómez, PhD. The Power
of Peace is available as a twelve-page booklet from PsycHealth Ltd.,
http://nospank.net/pop.htm (accessed March 2011).

Phoenix Children's Hospital
Principles and Practices of Effective Discipline—Advice for Parents
A brochure companion to *The Report on Physical Punishment in the United States: What Research Tells Us about Its Effects on Children*, by Elizabeth Gershoff, PhD,
http://www.phoenixchildrens.com/PDFs/effective_discipline_brochure.pdf (accessed July 2011).

Save the Children Sweden
Positive Discipline: What It Is and How to Do It
A brochure written by Joan Durrant, PhD, and published by Save the Children Sweden,
http://www.stophitting.com/pdf/PositiveDiscipline-WhatItIsandHowToDoIt.pdf (February 2011).

The University of Maine Cooperative Extension
Discipline that Works: The Ages and Stages Approach
The University of Maine Cooperative Extension,
http://www.umext.maine.edu/onlinepubs/PDFpubs/4140.pdf (accessed July 2011).

ACKNOWLEDGMENTS: Thank you to all the children and families who have contributed to this book and to the Guernsey County (Ohio) Court-Appointed Special Advocates (CASA), Rosemont Center (Columbus, Ohio), and St. Angela School (Chicago, Illinois) for their special participation.

Many recommendations for parents came from the Guernsey County CASA in Ohio.

Guernsey County CASA has annually conducted an essay contest for SpankOut Day April 30 during child abuse and prevention month. This began with a grant, but we have continued the event after that. The young people impressed us and made it very difficult to select "winners," as they are all winners in our eyes. Our thanks to SpankOut Day April 30 for offering us a fantastic event." —Jean Stevens, Director, and Kathy Walters, Volunteer Coordinator Guernsey County CASA

Thank you to PsychHealth Ltd., Evanston, Illinois, for supporting writing, and drawing contests about spanking and alternatives for children.

Made in the USA
Charleston, SC
03 October 2011